The Adventure
And
The Legend of Council Mountain

By Stephen Mehen

This is a fictional story only the names have been changed to protect the author from physical abuse.

CHAPTER ONE

THE OLD MAN IN THE PARK

The sun just peeked its head over the left shoulder of Council Mountain. The sun's rays stretched across the steel blue carpet as the dust particles danced in the newborn light. "Thump, thump," was the sound from the beating of the rug by Chocolate, the eighty-five pound Labrador, of the same color, lying next to the bed. The result was the dancing dust particles in the shimmering rays of the sun.

Sean Conroy lay sound asleep in his bed, his head half covered by the bedding – not hearing a sound. Finally, Chocolate jumped to his feet. Thoughts of hunting, swimming, running or playing raced through Chocolate's mind. "It's time to get going. I need to get Sean up," is what Chocolate was thinking. Sean then just rolled over so his face was at the edge of the bed facing Chocolate. Slurp, slobber, lick, lick, went Chocolate's tongue all over Sean's face. "Go away, Chocolate," cried Sean as he rolled back over. That was not what Chocolate wanted to happen. So

Plan Number Two was to be executed. Chocolate leapt up on Sean's bed. Slurp, slurp, slobber, lick, lick went Chocolate's tongue on Sean's face again as Chocolate's eighty-five pound body stood over Sean. "Okay, okay, Chocolate," Sean yelled. "I'll get up."

Sean slowly sat up and swung his legs over the side of the bed. Chocolate jumped off and raced down the stairs of the loft where Chocolate and Sean slept. Sean peeked over the railing that looked over the family room through the dining area and into the kitchen. The smell of brewing coffee was filling the house.

Mrs. Conroy was in the kitchen rattling pots and pans. Chocolate was already in the kitchen wagging his five pound tail, thinking he would get fed soon. Sean stumbled down the stairs, half asleep, into the bathroom. He brushed his teeth, combed his hair and went into the dining room. "What's for breakfast, Mom?" "Oatmeal, English muffins and some bacon." "Not that instant stuff!" Sean exclaimed. "No, you can smother the real McCoy with whatever junk you like."

Just then, Mr. Conroy came in with the fresh milk he got from Daisy, their Jersey cow. He said, "Well, Mom, Jose' got the last hay in the barn for the winter." "Good," Mrs. Conroy said, "We should start getting ready for fall roundup." "That's right, Mom. School starts soon right after Labor Day. Then it's weaning time." There was silence for a minute, then Sean said, "Oh, no! Not school so soon." "Oh, yes! You will be in the seventh grade." Mrs. Conroy explained. "It's time to start growing up. You think that will ever happen, Sean?" Sean said nothing. He just kept eating his oatmeal with cinnamon, sugar and fresh milk from Daisy.

Sean had just finished his breakfast when his cell phone rang. His mother had given him a cell phone so she could keep track of him. He was always somewhere he wasn't supposed to be. "Hi, Rory." Sean answered. "Meet you in the park in town where the old steam tractors are." "Okay." Rory answered.

The Conroys had moved to Idaho from California because the property tax on the ranch his great-grandfather homesteaded in 1849 was so high, they couldn't afford to run cattle on it anymore.

So they sold out and moved. The ranch was in North County, San Diego. It wasn't far from the ocean and Moonlight Beach where Sean learned to surf. So, when Sean got to Idaho, the transition to snowboarding was a piece of cake.

Rory's father was a lawyer who made a ton of money defending industry from wacko environmentalists when they made false claims in order to somehow make money from little old ladies on the East coast who had no idea what the cattle industry was all about, but had a soft heart for a sad story. The O'Brien's, Rory's family, were from North County San Diego area as well. Mr. O'Brien was a team roper with Sean's father in California. He retired early to become a cattle rancher. The O'Brien's bought the old Frasean Ranch across the road from the Conroys.

Sean asked his mother if he could meet Rory in the park. "Okay," his mother said. "But take Chocolate with you. He is driving me nuts." As if Sean was going to leave him home. Town was only three-quarters of a mile away.

Sean got his new BMX bike out of the barn and with Chocolate leading the way, they took off up the driveway that lead to the highway and then to town. Rory was already at the park with his black Labrador "Licorice". They both climbed up onto one of the steam tractors where they always planned their great adventures. Rory said, "Stacy called and said she would meet us here." Sean replied, "How come? What does she want." "I don't know," Rory said. "Most likely some girly gossip." "I will bet you it is about the new teacher we will have this year in the seventh grade." Sean said "You do know school starts soon." Rory replied," Yea, I know. My mom keeps saying I better get prepared for school in a few weeks. Summer is almost over."

Just about that time, Stacy arrived with her long auburn hair in a ponytail. "Hi, guys." Stacy shouted from the ground to the boys on the tractor.

Stacy climbed on the tractor immediately and said "Guess what?" Sean replied, "Oh, no. Now what?" "My mom said there is a new teacher in town," Stacy said. Sean and Rory both grinned at each other. "She is from New York City, is very excited to learn all about the west and is going to teach seventh grade." Rory chimed in, "Oh, boy, this is going to be fun. I bet she is green as grass and has trouble telling the difference between beans and wild honey." Sean replied, "What is her name?" Stacy said, "Miss Green." Rory replied, "Oh, boy. That fits." Stacy explained, "She is just out of college." Rory laughed, "That's even better." The boys started to giggle. Then Sean said, "Is she in town yet?" Stacy replied, "Yea, she is staying at Mrs. Bonny's house – you know, the principal – until she can find a place to live."

Miss Green got her BS in teaching from Columbia University in New York City. She grew up in the Bronx with great parents from Wales, England from a poor coal mining town. She was only five years old when she arrived in New York. She was very athletic, going through school playing basketball, soccer, even field and ice hockey. She was also a cheerleader. One time entered a beauty contest in which she came in second. She was very personable and good-looking, besides being talented both musically and in art. Adventure for her was the name of the game.

An old man sat on the bench, not far from the old steam tractors where Sean, Rory and Stacy were meeting. This was their favorite place to plan new exciting adventures. Chocolate and Licorice (Rory's black lab), had made a new buddy of the old man. The old man with his bib overalls, a gray beard, a BSU baseball hat, t-shirt, semi-long gray hair and holding a cane, sat petting both dogs at the same time. Then he motioned to the kids, "Come here and I will tell you a story." The children climbed down from the tractor and approached the old man unafraid. If Chocolate and Licorice licked him, he must be okay. Their parents had warned them of funny-looking strangers.

The old man said "Sit down." They sat down on the ground next to the dogs. He began. "A long time ago, there was a ring of very old-growth ponderosa trees. Every summer, the Indians from the north – the Nez Perce, and the Indians from the south – the Shoshone, would come to this area to have a council. Hence, the name of this town Council. The Nez Perce (French name meaning "man who carries a purse") would bring shells they got from trading with the Cayuse on the great Columbia River who got them from the Coastal Indians. They would bring baskets, leather goods, dried salmon and their famous horse – the Appaloosa for trading. The Shoshone from the south came with clay pots and other items for trade. They would also have games for all the people to compete in, especially horse races. The elders would meet in the ring of trees and smoke the peace pipes and make treaties about hunting grounds, fishing areas and agreements not to wage war against each other. They would also discuss what to do about the white-men coming to the area or passing through."

He also told them about the big breakup of the yearly council that had been tradition for hundreds of years. He said, "The Shoshone caught the NezPerce cheating in the great horse race that was held in what is now called Indian Valley." Sean asked, "How did they cheat in a horse race?" The old man replied, "No one is exactly sure. There are many myths as to what it was. One theory was that the Nez Perce had a mineral substance they dug from the ground and fed to the horses just before the race. Some say it was sodium bicarbonate. Then the Shoshone stole some from the Nez Perce and fed it to some of their horses. If they did not run them, the horses died."

The old man kept telling the story. "That caused the breakup of the council after hundreds of years. Do you kids want a great adventure? See if you can find the ring of trees. Some say that the Shoshone cut them down and others say that when the loggers came they cut them down. Some say it was the great fire of 1910. They were supposed to be north of Council along the Weiser River, but no one has ever found them." The children remained silent for a long time. Then the old man said, "I have to go now. Good luck. I hope you find the ring. They say there were caves nearby where the gold the Indians found was stored. They tried to make jewelry out of the gold. Some say the Nez Perce wore shells and arrowheads plated with gold." The old man stood up, grabbed his cane and hobbled off into town and disappeared.

CHAPTER TWO

JOSE'

South of the San Rafael Valley in southern Arizona, along the Mexican border lies an old Spanish Land Grant established in 1549 by Spanish aristocrats from Andalusia, Spain. Headquarters were at Canelo, Arizona in 1549 until 1863 when the Gateston purchase split off Southern Arizona from Mexico. The headquarters then moved to halfway between Locheal, Arizona and Cananea, Mexico. On the Arizona side, the Land Grant San Ignatius Del Babicomer, the San Rafael, the Baca Float and the Santa Cruz were what were left in Southern Arizona of Spanish land grants.

Jose's father was the lead Vaquero for the 300,000 plus acre rancho renamed the Santo Francisco. The Santo Francisco was owned by the Fembrace family from Mexicali, Mexico of Supermarket enterprises in Northern Mexico. Jose' was born at the headquarters and went through the 8th grade at the ranchero's grade school. High School was in Cananea – too far away for a day trip and his family did not have enough money for boarding school.

They say Jose' was born on a caballo (horse) with a reata in his hands. By the age of 12 he was as an accomplished vaquero as his father. He soon could run his own crew. On the rancho, he learned to drive almost anything from pickups to 18 wheelers by age 10.

During fall round up, when he was 17, Jose' was running a crew close to the Arizona border just south of Locheal, Arizona. A border patrol from the USA came into camp one evening in a 4-wheel drive Jeep. He was a friend of Jose's family. Jose' knew him well. He explained that some of the rancho's cattle was on the other side of the border. He gave Jose' permission to go to the Mark Buttress Ranch to gather the strays. The Buttress Ranch was a 7000 acre ranch split from the Old Green Cattle Company which was part of the original Land Grant in the San Rafael Valley. The strays were easily identified because the Santa Francisco ran a commercial outfit of mixed Corrientes, Brahma, and some English breeds, mostly Hereford, Angus and Shorthorn. The border patrol knew the rancho brand and earmark. The brand was a c double bar cross (C--+) left side and a swallow fork left ear.

Mr. Buttress was there at first light to meet Jose' and his crew to gather the cattle and help sort off the strays. The brand inspector from Arizona was also there to make sure the Mexican cattle not only were the right ones, but to check for health problems. The Arizona State Veterinarian was on hand after the cattle were sorted off. The Buttress cattle were put through the chute, scratched for Texas tick fever, and then jumped through the dipping vat. The Mexican cattle were just jumped through the dipping vat. They were then loaded in an 18 wheeler cattle truck.

Everything was clean. Mark Buttress was so impressed with Jose's ability to handle his crew and the cattle; he not only thanked him up and down, but offered him a job. Of course, Jose' refused and thanked Mr. Buttress. Jose' loaded the cattle and drove back to camp on the other side of the border. That night after the crew was fed, the horses fed, and the dogs got the dinner scraps and some dog chow, Jose' could not stop thinking about the job offer. So many of the kids Jose' went to grade school with had crossed the border illegally to work in the USA hoping to maybe become citizens of the US. They also made 3 to 10 times more money than they could in Mexico. Some had stayed and some had come back to Mexico with enough money to go to the university or buy a home and retire.

After the fall roundup was over, Jose' was sent to Mexicali driving a cattle truck to deliver a load of steers to the big feed lot Nutrimentos, which was owned by Armondo Galago, a relative of the Fembrace's. He got a day pass to visit Calexico, California. He walked across the border and went through all the stores and saw how the Americans lived.   They lived much better than in Mexico. He saw how clean the town was kept and how open everything was. He made up his mind that he was leaving for the US.

Back at the rancho a few weeks later, when the shipping and round-up were over and the cattle were turned out waiting for calving in the spring, Jose' told his mother of his plan to work for Mr. Buttress. She cried at first, but wanted the best for her son. His father was disappointed but sometimes wished he had jumped the line also.

Jose' took a pickup and a horse and drove to the border, but did not dive into the US. He rode his horse to the Buttress ranch to find Mark Buttress. He lived in Tucson, but was told he could stay with Shorty and Iness until Mr. Buttress returned. Mark had called Shorty that day and said he would be at the Ranch the next day.

Mark Buttress hired Jose' right away and proceeded to fill out all the paperwork to get Jose' a green card (work permit). He then filed them in Tucson and pulled the important strings to get Jose' at the head of the line. Mark's father was an ex-governor of Arizona. Jose' spent that winter learning Mark Buttress' operation. The Buttress Ranch ran cows and calves in Arizona and steers in Idaho in the summer. Jose' got his green card and a CDL (Commercial Driver's License) that winter.

In May the snow had melted and the grass was coming fast. Mark loaded Jose' with 100 steer calves on one of his cattle trucks and Mark drove another rig with 102 calves averaging 500 lbs and they were off to New Meadows, Idaho. That summer Jose' learned

how to fish and white water raft. Mark told him he was to stay the

winter where he learned to snowboard at Brundage Mountain. He

now was a true Idahoan.

CHAPTER THREE

FIRST DAY OF SCHOOL

The phone rang in the kitchen at the Conroy Ranch. Mrs. Conroy answered. "Yes, Rory, Sean is up. When he finishes his breakfast you two can ride your bikes to school." Sean ate his breakfast and proceeded up the driveway to the highway to meet Rory. They got to school early so they could see all their friends and tell of the great adventures they had that summer, about what they were going to do during hunting season and round up that fall, but mostly about the new school teacher from New York City.

Plans were in the making to break Miss Green in the Idaho way. The bell rang and the kids were off to class. Miss Green introduced herself. She told about her life in New York City.

Meanwhile at the ranch, Jose' let Chocolate out of the kennel. Knowing that Sean was gone, Chocolate was off to town. He recognized Sean's bike in the bike stand where he always parked it. Mrs. Bonnie, the principal, came out the front door to get something out of her car. Chocolate charged in, down the hall, sniffing all scents until he got to the 7th grade door. He was a bird dog, you know. Miss Green had left the door open a crack. In the door he went, banging his tail on everything, looking for Sean. The whole class yelled, "Chocolate". The class then went nuts. Chaos was on. Miss Green panicked. She had no idea what to do. She had never had an 85 lb Labrador in her class in New York City. Meanwhile, Mrs. Bonnie was running down the hall screaming, "How did that darn dog get in here?" Miss Green had jumped upon her desk as if a vicious wolf was about to eat her. Mrs. Bonnie's husband was a duck hunter and they had labs. She rushed in yelling, "Sean, get Chocolate out of here." It seems that Chocolate had a habit of coming to school in years before.

Sean and Rory were both laughing so hard they were just standing there. Stacy screamed, "Way to go, Chocolate." Mrs. Bonnie yelled, "Sean, get Chocolate by the collar and get into my office. Miss Green, get off that desk and stop crying and grow up. You also get in my office."

Off to the office they went. Mrs. Bonnie got on the phone to Mrs. Conroy. "Get up here to school and get that darn dog home." Rory and Stacy followed them down the hall but just stayed at the open door of Mrs. Bonnie's office. Mrs. Bonnie then said, "All of you sit down." Miss Green was still sobbing a little. "Sean, you and the dog get outside. Rory and Stacy, get back to class."

Mrs. Conroy pulled into school parking lot. Sean loaded Chocolate into the pickup and she left for the ranch before Mrs. Bonnie could chew her out. When she was leaving she told Sean, "It is not your fault. Maybe I should talk to Jose' about letting Chocolate out of the kennel while you are in school. Maybe we should have Miss Green over for dinner."

Back in the office Mrs. Bonnie got control of herself and explained to Miss Green, "This is not New York City. Don't panic. Get used to western ways because you most likely ain't seen anything yet!"

Jose' had been in the USA now for 10 years. He became a US citizen and when Mr. Buttress sold his ranch in Meadows Valley last year he decided to stay in the great state of Idaho. Mr. Buttress knew the Conroys and got Jose' the job with the Conroys. Jose' had only been at the Conroys for about a year. He blended in so well with the family to the point of almost being a family member. He now was in his late 20's. He stood about 6' 1" to 6' 2" and weighed 180 lbs, taking on the look of a dashing caballero from the 1920's movie era; quite handsome.

CHAPTER FOUR

THE DINNER

Mrs. Conroy discussed with Mr. Conroy what they should do for dinner when they invited Miss Green to the ranch as a dinner guest. They thought maybe they should also invite Mrs. Bonnie, Rory, Stacy and the O'Briens. They decided to have a barbeque on the deck behind the house under the 100 year old apple tree.

They invited everyone on the list. Mrs. Bonnie was the only one who could not come because she lived in McCall and had other commitments. As a school administrator in Council, she still had some influence in McCall and needed to butt heads with the somewhat backwards, non-progressive city council that night, so she begged off.

The barbeque was in September on a Friday night starting about 6 p.m. The thorn bush had turned red and all the apples had been picked or fallen off the big tree in the middle of the deck and were fed to the hogs and some to the horses.

A long table was set up that would seat about 10 – four on each side- on long benches and one on each end. Rory brought his little sister, Vickie. Vickie was in the 2nd grade, was seven years old, but always wanted to play with the big kids.

Mr. Conroy wanted to introduce Miss Green to western BBQ so he cooked beef ribs, pork ribs and lamb chops. He also, cooked hamburgers for the kids just in case they wanted the same old thing. Mrs. Conroy cooked some good Idaho potatoes, made a big salad and baked some Basque bread. Miss Green arrived early to help Mrs. Conroy in the kitchen but had no idea what to do. She was very limited in her cooking ability. In other words, she was as green as spring grass when she was in the kitchen.

Mr. and Mrs. Conroy sat on the ends of the long table. Rory and Stacy sat on one side across from Sean and little Vickie. Mr. and Mrs. O'Brien sat across from each other. Jose' sat across from Miss Green at the end where Mrs. Conroy sat.

Everybody got a little of everything, except little Vicki. But she got a hamburger and half of an Idaho baked potato and a little salad. The O'Briens brought Licorice, their black lab, so Chocolate

was let out of the kennel. They quickly took off for the Weiser River

that ran through the meadow.

The conversation quickly turned to the up and coming

Round Up. Jose' was paying no attention. He just kept staring at

Miss Green and mumbling something in Spanish. She, having

studied Spanish at the University in New York City, picked up what

he was mumbling. She began speaking in Spanish to him and he

spoke back. Mrs. Conroy, who was very observant, caught on to

her goggle eyes and his grinning and squirming around. She said to

herself, "Oh, here we go!"

Sean, Rory, and Stacy stopped talking and stared and

listened to the Spanish wondering what this was all about. The

Round Up conversation stopped and all listened.

This went on for a little bit longer until all of a sudden,

Chocolate and Licorice showed up. The smell of the BBQ had

drifted down to the river. Thoughts ran through their minds "free

bones." Upon the deck their big tails wagged everywhere. "OK,

OK," Mr. Conroy yelled. "Come with me you guys. I've a present for you." BONES.

A burst of wind blew a few apples into the yard that had been missed when Jose' picked the tree. There was thunder and lightning. The team of draft horses was just outside the gate of the yard so Sean got up from the table and let them in. They quickly cleaned up the apples and went back out the gate. The team was used to pull the hay in wagons in the winter to feed the cattle in the Meadows. They were both black cross breeds with mostly draft horse bred into them.

Everyone got back to the table for dessert - homemade ice cream and chocolate cake.

The conversation turned back to Round Up and both Mr. Conroy and Mr. O'Brien invited Miss Green to help. It would start the first of October. Sean and Rory giggled and whispered back and forth, "Boy is this going to be fun." Mr. O'Brien heard it and said to both of them, "Cool it. I better not catch you guys pulling any tricks." The giggles went on as their little minds were working overtime.

When dessert was over, the kids were summoned into the kitchen to wash the dishes, supervised by Mrs. Conroy.

The other adults retired to the living room for more discussion about Round Up and the calf market. The market was up this year and both Mr. Conroy and Mr. O'Brien had been on the phone to buyers looking for the best price.

After about an hour of listening to all the cattle talk, Miss Green got bored and excused herself. Jose' jumped up and asked her if he could drive her home. She had ridden her bike from town to the ranch – only about a mile away.

Why not? She thanked both the Conroys and the O'Briens. Jose' put her bike in the back of the pickup and drove to town. As Jose' and Miss Green left for town, both sets of parents said at the same time, "Oh. Oh!" An hour long discussion went on about what was happening.

Sean, Rory, Stacey and little Vickie had gone outside to play with the dogs. Again there was thunder and lightning. They came back in and sat on the floor, and began to fall asleep. "Time to go home, Rory and Vickie." They left with the dog for their ranch.

CHAPTER FIVE

ROUND-UP

October first came around real fast. Everyone on both ranches – the Conroy's and the O'Brien's – was busy getting everything together. Sean and Rory were to make sure the horses were gathered up and close to the central corral system. Sean helped Rory at his ranch and then they went to the Conroy Ranch. Sean wanted to make sure that the old strawberry roan mare was in the Remuda. Sean always rode her during round up. Roanie, as she was named, was trained as a cuttin' horse. She was Poco Bueno on the top side and Three Bars on the bottom. Although she was long retired from competition she was still one of the best cow horses on the ranch. Even at 18 years old she had a reputation far and wide. Some old timers would say she was such a good cuttin' horse she could sort piss ants out of sorghum molasses on a cold January day. Now, that's a cuttin' horse.

When the horses were all gathered and fed some hay, Sean and Rory sat up in the hay loft and began to talk about roundup.

The conversation soon turned to the reality that Jose' had invited Miss Green to come help. The plan soon turned to how to break Miss Green in the right way. Greenhorn tricks were common during roundup. One time someone started a manure fight, the tender foot from L. A., California took off. Some say he went back to L. A. that day.

The next day at school during recess, Sean, Rory, Stacy and a few others made a plan of attack and were sworn to secrecy. They knew Jose' would not let them do the dirty tricks so they had to keep it simple.

Neighbors of the O'Brien's came to help and since the Conroys ran with big Mike, the county commissioner, he and his crew came to help. He also ran on Council Mountain, on a small permit with the O'Brien's. Big Mike had good cow dogs, Queensland Healers and Australian Sheppards, so the Labs were left at home. The local veterinary came to preg check and brought a helper. The cattle were gathered off of the east face of Cutty Mountain on the Conroy side first. Everything went smoothly. No tricks yet. Then they moved to the O'Brien Ranch. The cattle were gathered off the west face of Council Mountain and moved to the corrals on Cottonwood Creek. The fun was about to begin.

Miss Green had some horse riding training at a stable north of New York City, so she was mounted on a gentle gelding and helped with the gathering. She road English back east so the transition was easy to a western saddle.

As they were moving the cows and calves toward the corrals, Jose' motioned to both Mr. Conroy and Mr. O'Brien to come over to him. He had found fresh tracks of a wolf about 6" or 7" long. "This is a big one," he said. Both Mr. O'Brien and Mr. Conroy looked at each other and at the same time said, "Wonder how many we lost this year." Last year both ranches lost 15 and 18 calves respectively to wolf kill.

The most expensive part is that the wolves will run the cattle. Even if they don't kill any calves, the cows will lose a body condition score and weaning weights will be lower. Wolves will run cattle just for fun or in training the pup's survival skills.

Miss Green rode over to where the men were and got first hand information on how wolves had cost ranchers big bucks. It can cost anywhere from $50 a head to over $100 a head to put back a body condition score. Before wolves, the cows would gain a body condition score through the summer on the good grass. Miss Green is or was a real brainwashed Greenie. Time will tell?

The cattle were moved into the corral system designed by Dr. Temple Grandin from CSU, and sorting was started. In the sorting alley the cows went to a chute area and the calves to a pen system. The veterinary was at the chute ready to start preg checking. Sean and Rory made sure that Miss Green got the tail job. She was to hold the tail of the cow so Doc could arm the cow for pregnancy. Mr. Conroy, Mr. O'Brien, and Big Mike's cows were then sorted as they came out of the chute; culls one way and pregnant cows the other way, according to whose they were. A count was taken to see how many strays might still be on the forest permit.

The first cow came through; Miss Green grabbed the messy tail and immediately screamed, "Yuck." She let go of the messy tail which then came around, the switch at the end of the tail, full of you know what, got her right in the face. Another "Yuck" and a rush to the water trough, then crying and big tears. "OK," Mr. Conroy said, "you guys, that was a dirty trick. Now all three of you over to the sorting alley and sort the steers from the heifers."

Jose' took the three over to the alley. Jose' would do the sorting. Miss Green was the chaser, Sean on one gate for the steers, and Rory on another for the heifers. Big Mike's calves were by's. They moved about 20 or 30 calves into the alley up against a cross gate. Jose' peeled off one calf at a time and would call out steer, heifer or by. The first few came through, and then Miss Green said, "How do you tell if it is a steer or a heifer?" Rory explained in a loud voice, "The finger test. Take two fingers, lift up their tail and poke. If one finger doubles back, it's a steer." Miss Green looked at Rory first very quizzically, then in disgust. As Jose' was explaining that a smooth belly was a heifer and hair hanging down the middle of the belly was a steer, Sean in a low voice said to Rory, "You want to pass the 7th grade?"

A few more came through. Jose' asked Sean and Rory if they were getting a count. Miss Green then asked, "How do you count these things when they come by so fast?" Rory again jumped on the answer, "Count the legs and divide by 4." Miss Green again looked like she was being put on. Then everyone laughed. Jose' then said we will get a count later. The sorting went on. Two steers and one heifer came through. Jose' yelled, "Stop them! Bring them back!" Miss Green was panicked. She tried to stop them but lost one. Both Sean and Rory yelled "Don't weaken Miss Green. Oh oh. Too late." Rory stopped the one and Sean shut his gate and moved the calves back to Jose'. After about 200 calves were sorted off of the bunch, the alley got slippery so each time a mix of steers and heifers came through the boy's would yell "don't weaken" and Miss Green would try her hardest but would slip and fall on the slick alley floor, The boys would giggle.

After a few more slip and falls, Miss Green was covered with you know what. The boy's thought that was great. Jose' said, "Miss Green, go help the ladies prepare for lunch. Send Stacy or somebody back here.

The lunch bell was rung. Everyone tried to stop for lunch and resume afterwards. At lunch the boys started to plan for the afternoon but learned that Miss Green went home to take a bath. Nobody knew if she would come back. When she left, nobody knew if she was mad or what. So the boys decided to forget the plan. Rory started to worry if he would pass the 7th grade. She showed up for dinner that evening all clean, ready to help with the dishes. She commented to someone, "This ranch life has more to it than meets the eye.

CHAPTER SIX

THE FIRST SNOW

Roundup was over. The cows lost a body condition score, the count was short, and the calves were lighter. But the better market saved the day.

Both Mr. Conroy and Mr. O'Brien went to Boise to the U. S. Fish and Wildlife to see Ranger Pete. They wanted to file for some money for their loss, but with no actual proof of a wolf kill or a ranger investigation, there was no chance. Mr. O'Brien, being a lawyer, got copies of the laws and found out quickly that all laws were in favor of the wolf. It was like wolves were superior citizens to real people. Ranger Pete explained that they knew wolves had moved into the Council Mountain area but not just where they saw the tracks. He explained that there were an abundance of black bears there and wolves seem to not want to be in the same area.

Every year both the Conroy and the O'Brien parents go home to Encinitas, California after round up. Miss Green volunteered to baby sit Rory and little Vickie at the O'Brien Ranch.

Jose' stayed with Sean at the Conroy Ranch. When the snow

started Jose' fed at both Ranches until the parents got home.

One night in the first week of November it started to snow.

Sean called Rory, "It is supposed to be a big dump according to the

weather channel." Rory answered, "Yea, you got your snowboard

waxed?" "No," said Sean, "I better get it done." "Me, too," said

Rory, "See you at school in the morning."

It was Friday the next day and then the weekend. Friday

morning Sean got up earlier than normal. It was still dark outside.

Jose' was already out feeding. Sean turned on the Boise Channel to

see if he could find the weather. No luck, so he went out on the

front porch. "Holy Cow, look at that!" Sean yelled. There was a real

big dump. Jose' came in and said, "There are three to four feet

some places. You better call Rory." Just then the phone rang. It

was Miss Green. She explained that Mrs. Bonnie called and said

that it was a snow day, no school. She asked Jose' if he was on his

way over to feed and clear the driveway. Sean said, "Let me talk to

Rory. Let's plan a great adventure." "OK," responded Rory.

Sean road on the skip loader over to Rory's with Jose' as he plowed his way over. Jose' and the boys got the cattle fed as Miss Green and little Vickie cooked some breakfast. At breakfast Jose' mentioned that up the Cottonwood Creek Road there were hunters in the cabin that an outfitter rented from the Forest Service. He said he better call Big Mike, County Commissioner, and tell him that the county better plow the road up to that cabin. Jose' called and Mike said it would be late in the day. Other roads had to be plowed first.

Just then the light came on. Both Sean and Rory had the same thought at the same time. They excused themselves from the breakfast table and went to Rory's room where they started to put the plan together.

Later that day, Rory road with Sean and Jose' back to the Conroy Ranch on the skip loader. Stacy showed up on cross-country skis and the three discussed the plan. All they had to do was con Jose' into being part of it. That was not going to be easy.

The three cornered Jose'. They let Stacy lead into the conversation.

"Jose', sweetie, we need some practice on our snow board technique. You think you could drive us up to the hunting cabin on Cottonwood Creek so we can board down?" All three at one time said "Oh, come on, Jose', you're so cool, we just know you will."

"By the way, how are you and Miss Green getting along?" asked Rory with a big grin.

Jose' turned a little red in the face. All three laughed. Jose' got the message. "OK, after feeding in the morning everyone meet at Rory's place." Jose' explained.

Friday afternoon the sun came out and the temperature went back to normal for the first part of November. The snow stared to melt a little bit. Jose' told Miss Green of the plan. She was reluctant at first, but said, "Ok. But you are responsible." The next morning the temperature was freezing, but was soon to be warming up quickly.

Jose' had no idea that the kids planned to pack their skins in their backpacks and not board down the snow packed road back to Rory's. The skins allowed the boarder to go up hill. They piled into the 4-wheel drive pickup after feeding and headed up Cottonwood Creek Road. They passed the Cottonwood Creek corrals where the roundup was. As they went by, Jose' said, "I will meet you guys here. Stay close to the road." They went on up to the hunters cabin. Jose' let them off and went back to the corrals. The three took off down the side of the road about 50 yards and stopped. Sean said, "Is Jose' out of sight?"

"Yes," Rory answered.

They put their skins on their boards and pumped up the mountain. They were not far from the tree line. They got up to where they needed to be to follow what they thought was a trail which they had moved the cows and calves down during roundup.

They stopped and took off their skins. Sean led the way, with Rory and Stacy behind. Sean soon lost what he thought was the trail back to the corrals. He was veering to the north where there was a big lava flow, from thousands of years ago. Not far below the tree line to the north of where they were to be, Sean came to a quick stop and sat down on his butt, which was common for snow boarders. About three or four feet in front of him was a fifteen foot cliff. He eased over the top of the cliff and looked over. Soon Rory and Stacy did the same.

In total amazement all three stared down the cliff. About 30 feet in front of the cliff was a mass of huge ponderosa trees with a four foot opening into what appeared to be a ring of tall trees.

All three looked at each other in wonderment, their minds turned back to that day in the park when the old man told them the story of the ring of trees, the annual council of the Nez Perce and the Shoshone Indians, the agreements between the tribes, the dances, the trades and the horse races. All of these festivities they did for hundreds of years before the white man came into Idaho. Sean looked around for a way down. The cliff tapered down to just a few feet high to the south. They agreed to follow Sean down to the low spot and then side hop back to the opening.

As they side hopped on their boards they noticed caves going back into the cliff. There must have been 20 or 30 openings in the cliff. They came to the opening in the trees and stopped, staring both at the caves and the ring of trees. Sean got off his board and went into the cave at front of the opening in the ring of trees. He soon came out.

He said, "Be quiet you guys. There are whole bunches of bears sleeping in there."

Stacy soon whispered, "You guys know bears hibernate in winter." Sean and Rory answered, "Da." As they entered the ring of trees, their minds wondered about the many council that were held there. The teepees pitched with smoking of the peace pipes. The ring was about 30 feet in diameter. The trees were very close together; about four or five feet in diameter and very, very tall. There was another opening on the other side directly across from the one they just came in. It appeared that it was set up so the sun in the east at sunrise came in the opening where the kids came in. The west opening received the sun at sunset. They wondered if the

Indians planted the trees long ago or did they just find what Mother Nature made herself.

They went out the west opening and planned to return when the snow melted in the spring or into summer when not so much work was to be done and they were out of school for summer vacation. They could see part of town from there and Sean figured out how to get back to the corrals. They made a pact that they would only tell parents and not spread it all over town.

They wound through the trees always working southwest toward the corrals until they reached Jose' waiting in the pickup. "Where the hell have you guys been?" Jose' asked. "Oh, we got lost for a while, but got back anyway," Sean explained. "We better get back before Miss Green gets upset at me," Jose' said.

If that bothered him like that, must be he was getting hooked on Miss Green. They took off for the O'Brien Ranch.

CHAPTER SEVEN

THANKSGIVING

Sean, Rory and Stacy, after arriving at the O'Brien's Ranch, went immediately into the barn before Miss Green could come out of the house. Rory kept his snowboard there so it was natural to go right in. They then made a pact to not tell anyone. Miss Green came out of the house with little Vickie behind with a very worried look on her face. She jumped Jose', "What happened, why are you guys so late?"

Jose' answered very calmly, sticking up for the kids, "We took a little side trip." Sean and Rory both took on a sigh of relief thinking, "Way to go Jose'!" Jose' had this twinkle in his eye as he smoothed over Miss Green. She also was twinkling back.

Thanksgiving was in a few weeks and the parents were now back. Fall turkey season just started and Jose' wanted to shoot a Tom for Thanksgiving. He had spotted some back up Hornet Creek a few days ago. He invited Miss Green to join him the coming weekend before Thanksgiving.

The first snow had mostly melted in the valleys but up high on the mountains was still very deep. Most wildlife had now moved down to the valley floor, so turkey hunting should be good.

That weekend early Saturday morning, Jose' picked up Miss Green in town and headed up Hornet Creek. Sean and Rory were not invited. Jose' knew better than to take Chocolate with him. He would scare all of the turkeys away.

Dressed in camouflage they hid themselves in the brush in a make shift blind. Then with turkey calls they began to call some toms in. The big toms with the long beards were tough to eat (cook right). The smaller ones or young ones were the best. They were gone all day and into the night before they returned. What went on? They did bag several small toms.

That Sunday, Jose' and Miss Green spent most of the day in the barn at the Conroy Ranch cleaning the birds. They went in and out of the barn, then in and out of Jose's bunk house all day into the night. What went on? Mrs. Conroy started to get the hint. The birds were picked and cleaned and kept in the ice box till Thanksgiving.

It was a short school week. Fall was in full swing. The leaves were mostly off the trees and the fall sun was far to the south, giving the mountains and valley that fall look of a different colored light. Mrs. Conroy planned a big Thanksgiving, since Jose' and Miss Green got so many turkeys. She had a special recipe for wild turkeys. So she invited the O'Brien's, Stacy and her Uncle Louie for dinner. Miss Green and Jose' on the morning before Thanksgiving took the turkeys out of the ice box. Under Mrs. Conroy's direction they put the birds in a #9 wash tub and made a brine solution of salt and sugar, then her secret ingredient - a bottle of white wine. Later that evening, Mr. Conroy and Jose' prepared the deep pit barbeque with hard wood burnt down to coals. The birds were prepared by stuffing a quarter pound of butter under the skin over the breast and legs, then salt and pepper added on the skin. They were then wrapped in tin foil and wet burlap and hung off the hot coals on a black iron pipe, covered with tin roofing and dirt to form a giant pressure cooker.

Thanksgiving morning Mr. Conroy and Jose' removed the turkeys from the pit. Mrs. Conroy, with the help of Miss Green, made Idaho potato salad, a big green salad and some vegetables. And some garlic bread. The O'Brien's, Stacy and her Uncle arrived at noon before the 1 pm dinner. The tables were set up on the deck under the 100 year old apple tree. It was a very beautiful sunny fall day.

The fall off the bone turkey meat was prepared and the meal was set on the tables. The adults sat at one table and the kids at another. Wine was served to the adults and non-alcohol wine to the kids. Mr. Conroy said grace and then Jose' asked if he could make a toast.

He stood up, raised his glass and then said," Josephine, will you marry me?"

Surprise, surprise! Miss Green turned red, stood up and yelled "Yes! I never thought you would ask." The silence was broken. Everyone clapped and cheered. She flung her arms around him then kissed him.

Sean then said, "Hey, Rory, Miss Green has a first name." Rory giggled then said "Wait until everyone at school finds out." Mischief was always on Rory's mind.

Mrs. Conroy asked," Jose' and Josephine, when is the big day?" Jose' answered, "We thought maybe in the spring. I first have to go to New York to meet her parents." Miss Green then responded, "They may come out west instead for they have never been in the west." Mrs. O'Brien said, "You guys better get a date soon so we can plan a big wedding. No running off to Las Vegas or Reno. No New York wedding, OK? Miss Green said, "No way, right here."

The Thanksgiving dinner went long after when it should have ended. The conversation went on and on about how the wedding would take place. The kids took the dogs and went to the river to scare up some ducks. Rory kept going over nick names for Miss Green.

CHAPTER EIGHT

SPRING TURNOUT

The next day at school Sean, Rory and Stacy spread Miss Green's first name all over school and the news about the wedding that would take place sometime soon. Rory started to tell everyone that Miss Green's new nickname was Jo-Bee since the kids in school picked up on the new name, it stuck.

That week it started snowing again and the school started up the ski and snow board club. Every weekend the bus took the club to Brundage Mountain Ski Hill for competitions and the Mighty Mites to the Little Ski Hill. This would go on all winter.

During Christmas vacation, Miss Green and Jose' went to New York to meet her parents. When they returned after New Years they announced that the wedding would be after spring turn out, the 9th of May, Mother's Day was the big day. That is when everything is green and the Camas flowers, sunflowers, and other native flowers are in bloom and snow is still high up on the peaks.

Jo-Bee was a better than most skier having skied New England for many years. Jose' taught her how to snowboard, which she picked up on quickly. One day Sean, Rory, Stacy, Jose' and Jo-Bee had a race from the top of Brundage down Main Street to the Lodge. Rory jumped out in the lead thinking he was great stuff until he got to the big sweeping curve into the Lodge. There he tried to be funny with jumping over a hump on the downhill side and grabbed air for about fifteen feet and lost balance landing on his back. Jo-Bee went flying by followed by Sean, Jose', and Stacy, way behind as usual. At the Lodge, Sean started to tease Rory. The fight was on. Jose' had to break them up.

Monday at school Sean asked Rory if he wanted to tell the class who won. Stacey yelled out "Jo-Bee". Rory tried to think of an excuse but whispered to Jake, a classmate, "I will get her next time."

The wedding would be at the Conroy Ranch in the yard.

The forest permits for both ranches started April 15th so branding and vaccinations had to be done beforehand. Jo-Bee fell in love with the baby calves. She was becoming a real Idahoan rancher and conservationist not a Mickey Mouse (greenie) environmentalist trying to destroy the western way of life.

April 15th came and everyone got horse back and started to move cattle up to the corrals on Cottonwood Creek for branding. There were the O'Briens, the Conroys and Big Mike and his crew. Branding was done the old fashioned way, by head and heeling the calf on horseback then worked right there on the ground. The first day the O'Brien calves were vaccinated and branded then moved to the mountain not to far up. The next day the Conroy calves were worked. Most of the Conroy cattle ran up the east side of Cuddy Mountain. So there were only a small number to work on the second day.

On that second day everyone had the afternoon off. So Sean, Rory, and Stacy decided after lunch to venture up the mountain to try to find the ring of trees. They went up the road then veered off the road to the northeast, trying to remember where they went because last fall everything was covered in deep snow. They worked their way up toward the tree line. They then came to a fence. Sean said, "There was no fence before was there?" Rory answered, "Boy, the snow must have been very deep last fall."

Sean said, "We never went any further when there was no snow because this must be where our permit ended." They followed up the fence where it ended up against a tall rock cliff. Sean said, "Stacy, hold my horse. I am going to climb this cliff to the bench above."

When he got up there he looked around and saw what looked like the cliff they were on in the fall to the north. He yelled down to Rory and Stacy, "Tie up the horses and come on up." Rory and Stacy climbed up the cliff. They hiked over to what they thought was where they saw the ring of trees. They arrived where they went down on their snow boards. The cliff they were on had dipped down into a ravine then came up the other side. There was the ring about 100 yards farther north. They went up the other side of the ravine to the top of the cliff so they could look down on the ring. When they got there they noticed down along the base of the cliff bears were going in and out of the caves where they hibernated all winter long. Also, there were many small baby bears. They noticed that the grass and brush was very tall, having not been grazed. Having not been grazed it could be fuel for a forest fire. Sean said to Rory and Stacy, "Why was the ring fenced off?" Rory answered, "I don't know, but I will bet Fish and Game did it to keep cattle away from the bears." Stacy tuned in, "I think you're right."

Sean wondered why the Fish and Game never said anything about the ring of trees. Maybe they never heard the legend. Most of them were from back East. Anyway, how could they know?

The three kids decided to keep the secret and headed back to the corrals. On the way back to the horses, Sean asked the other two kids if they noticed that a ways to the north of the caves there was a creek that flowed out of the last cave. Rory said, "I wonder if that is where Cottonwood Creek starts?"

All three of them wondered why nobody ever found the beginning of the creek. They got to the horses and headed back to the corrals where the rest of the crew was.

The camp cooks were starting dinner. The kids were very hungry but they needed to wash up in the creek. There in the creek bottom where Sean was washing his face something sparkled as the ripping water rushed by them as the sun was going down behind Cuddy Mountain. He reached down to the bottom of the creek and grabbed the shiny object and pulled it out of the water. It was the shape of a cross, but it was black except the tip of one end. The three kids all wondered what it was, so they finished washing their hands and faces then went back to camp to ask the others. Big Mike asked to see it. He rubbed it with his big fingers until some of the black started to come off. Big Mike said, "I think it is silver." He then kept rubbing until more and more of the black came off. There were no images or writing on it at all. Just a cross that was very crudely hammered into shape. At the top there was a hole that was shaped so a chain or rope could go through to hang somewhere. Big Mike explained that missionaries and Jesuits priests that came from Canada in the 1600's taught the Nez Perce the white man's religion.

Jose' asked to see it. He then explained that the Franciscans in Mexico did much the same to them in the 1500's, to the Yacques and the Apaches, most of which were gold or copper crosses. He gave it back to Sean and the kids and said, "Don't lose it, it is an artifact."

The three kids all looked at each other trying not to say anything that might give away their secret. That night they all wondered how the cross got where it was, if it was pushed by the water from the bear caves all the way down or if that was Cottonwood Creek that came out of the caves. Sean wondered if there were other artifacts inside the ring of trees. The snow covered it last fall and this spring the bears kept them from going inside the trees.

Around the campfire that night little was talked about the cross. Most of the conversation was about the wedding of Jose' to Jo-Bee to be on Mother's Day, May the 9th.

Everyone was excited about the coming event. Sean put the cross in his saddle bags and that is where it stayed until he got home.

The next day they moved the Conroy cattle up to their summer range, broke camp and went home. When Sean got home, he took the cross into the shop and put it on the buffing wheel. It got the rest of the tarnish off and shined up very bright. He then noticed that in the middle of the cross was a circle of dots on both sides. He wondered if that might signify the ring of trees. Maybe it belonged to a great chief or was a priest at one of the meetings. Back in the saddle bag the cross went.

Branding and turnout to the forest was now over. It was getting close to the wedding.

CHAPTER NINE

THE WEDDING TRICKS

At school everyone was abuzz about the wedding of Jo-Bee, even Mrs. Bonnie. Every trick Rory could think of to tease Jo-Bee, he pulled on her. One day Rory and Stacy collected about 100 plus or minus cans and tied them together on a clothes line and tied them under her car so she could not see them when she got in her car to go home from school. When she pulled out to the parking lot onto the highway she heard this big noise like her car was falling apart. Sheriff Rick was across the highway from the school because the busses were loaded with kids and parents picking up kids to go home. He was there every school day for safety. The highway was congested with kids, cars, and busses. The long stream of cans behind Miss Jo-Bee's car caused quite a sight, everyone looking out the windows of their vehicles, laughing. Sheriff Rick turned on his blinkie lights and pulled Miss Jo-Bee over, running over a few cans on the way. He was going to give her a ticket for littering until he figured out what was going on, as if the whole town didn't know.

He then asked if she just got married and where was Jose'. She replied that the wedding was not until two weeks from now. He gathered up the cans and put them in her trunk. She was not too happy. She went to the recycle center to deposit the cans.

The news of who did it was all over school. Mrs. Bonnie called Miss Jo-Bee, Rory and Stacy into her office. Rory and Stacy got detention for two weeks. They had to clean up all trash and sweep the parking lot after school. Miss Jo-Bee stayed in Mrs. Bonnie's office behind closed doors. Nobody knew what went on.

The two weeks before the wedding to be held at the Conroy Ranch was filled with preparations. Word spread and more than 500 guests were expected from as far south as Cambridge and Midvale and North to Riggins and McCall.

CHAPTER TEN

THE WEDDING

Mr. Conroy and Mr. O'Brien dug a BBQ pit to place 200 lbs of beef and 200 lbs of pork for an old fashioned covered pit BBQ. Volunteers agreed to put on a potluck with all kinds of dishes. There were also two dozen kegs of beer. Parking could prove to be a problem since the spring grass was coming and the ground was still soft from spring rains. Mrs. Bonnie agreed to let people park at the school and the Conroy's rented busses to go from the school to the Ranch and back. It took until midnight Saturday to finally be ready for the wedding.

Sunday morning, May 9th, Mother's Day, started with a beautiful sunrise over the still covered-with-snow way up high above the tree-line on Council Mountain. Sean was up early, about 6 am, all excited. He ran down stairs and called Rory. "Are you done feeding the horses?" Sean said. "Not yet." Rory replied. "Come on over when you finish," said Sean. Rory said, "I am not even up yet. Licorice and I will be there when I finish." "OK," said Sean.

Sean got dressed and went to the barn to feed. When he was finished he went into the tack room and got the silver cross out of his saddle bag. He knew that the priest from McCall was coming to do the wedding, so he wanted him to bless it. He took it to his room and hid it in his old toy box. Rory arrived and the two of them went to help. Big Mike, who volunteered to show people where to park cars along the ¾ mile long driveway to the ranch headquarters where the wedding would take place. The wedding was to start at 4 p.m. so people started to arrive at about noon. When the driveway was full, people were told to park at the school and take the busses. Big Mike and his hired hand went to hook up the blue roan mare that would pull the surrey with the fringe on top that would deliver the bride.

The mariachi band arrived from Caldwell and set up by the deck where the marriage would take place, under the 100 year old apple tree that grew through the deck. Father Henry "Hank"

O'Houlahan arrived and Sean ran up stairs and got the cross for Father Hank to bless. Father Hank blessed the cross then asked if he could use it in the ceremony. Sean said,"Yes." He did not know what the history of the silver cross was but remembered an old Gaelic custom he knew as a boy in Ireland that would bring good luck to the couple getting married.

The bride was dressing in Mrs. Conroy's bedroom along with the rest of the bridesmaids who were Mrs. Conroy, best lady, Mrs. O'Brien, Mrs. Bonnie and two other school teachers. Jose' was dressing in his bunk house in a traditional Mexican outfit loaned to him by one of the band members. His best man was Mr. Conroy, then Mr. O'Brien, Big Mike, Sean and Rory. Chocolate and Licorice were outfitted with little saddle bags that would carry a ring for Jo-Bee and a ring for Jose'. Stacy would lead the dogs on leashes behind little Vickie as the flower girl who would lead the procession.

The front yard and up the hillside to the north, across the creek and up the hillside to the south were loaded with people. The equipment on the cement slab was moved somewhere else and tables were set up for the reception. The bride was taken up the driveway to be loaded in the surrey and the band started to play 'Here Comes the Bride' Mexican style. Little Vickie started down the runway which was a 150' long red roll up rug. She spread flowers. The two dogs led by Stacy followed and then the wedding party. They lined up on the deck with Father Hank waiting for the bride. Jo-Bee's father, who flew out from New York City, was waiting for her part way down the runway. He helped her out of the surrey and walked her to the make shift alter on the deck.

Father Hank started the ceremony by holding up the silver cross Sean had loaned him and reciting an Irish good luck poem for the to-be-married couple that ended in "and may God hold you in the palm of his hand." He then asked for the rings. Stacy got the rings out of the doggie saddle bags and handed them to the presenters. As Father Hank said "Jose' do you take Josephine to be your lawful wedded wife" Chocolate barked. The crowd went nuts with laughter. As Father asked Josephine if she takes Jose' to be her lawful wedded husband, Licorice barked. Then both dogs started barking. The crowd roared. They both said yes, and put their rings on. Father Hank said," I pronounce you man and wife. You may now kiss your wife." The bride and groom walked down the red carpet followed by the dogs led by Stacy, little Vickie sprinkling flowers and then the wedding party.

Father Hank yelled out "Let the party begin" and everyone lined up to congratulate the couple and get some BBQ, beer and wine. The party would last into the night.

Sean asked his mother, "Where is Rory." She said, "Here comes Stacy, ask her." Stacy was giggling and said, "Follow me." They walked out towards the barn. Stacy was acting very funny so Sean asked, "You been drinking beer?" Stacy answered, "Yea, so has Rory. Follow me." They went behind the barn where Rory and a bunch of kids from school were sitting on hay bales laughing and giggling and drinking beer. Sean not understanding about alcohol effects asked "What's so funny." They all answered at one time, "Watch Chocolate and Licorice." The dogs had licked the beer off the top of the kegs and were stumbling all over the place. Sean said, "You guys are going to get in trouble." Rory answered, "Go get some beer. Oh, never mind, I will get it for you." Rory went through the barn on the way to where the kegs were and got a two pound coffee can that was used to feed grain to the horses. He went around to where the kegs were. When no one was looking he filled the can full of beer and went back to the kids. They all drank some more beer and started to plan what they were going to do to fix the newlyweds. The dogs went to the barn and fell asleep on the loose hay.

The kids went to the barn and got some of the livestock chalk, then headed to find the honeymoon car. They covered it with sayings from "Just Married" to "Help! He kidnapped me."

The party started to break up, the bride and groom left, and all of a sudden Rory threw up. The parents started to look for their kids. Rory's mother asked Sean, "Where is Rory?" Sean answered, "He fell asleep in your car." That raised questions and the parents started to talk to each other. She also could not find Licorice. Then the parents rounded up all the kids. Even Mrs. Bonnie got in the act.

The evil of drink at a young age was hammered home. Mrs. Bonnie said they were all on detention at school and would stay late to clean up at school. Rory, now out of the cab, smarted off by saying," What about the dogs? They get the same deal?" Mrs. Bonnie then responded," That's it Rory. Now you're really in trouble." His parents gave him so many extra chores to do he thought he would never get them all done.

They all went home. The party was over. The honeymoon was on. Everything went back to normal.

CHAPTER ELEVEN

THE COTTONWOOD CREEK FIRE

The kids got through their detention and spring proved to be very wet with rains coming every week for a few days. Then warm sunshine. A perfect spring. The grass for the cattle and the hay crops flourished. Sean and Rory helped Jose' and their fathers move the cattle up the mountain by moving the salt grounds. They also helped with irrigating the hay meadows. The spring rains lasted until about the 4th of July. Between cattle moves Sean, Rory and sometimes Stacy would get away from the adults and go to the ring of trees. By the middle of July the grass and brush was so high it was almost impossible to walk through. The bears had all left the caves to feed all summer. Since the circle of trees was fenced off the cattle could not graze that grass down. A huge problem if there was a fire. This amounts to fuel.

On the fourth of July the annual porcupine races were at the school. Sean got a garbage can from the barn the night before the 4th. Jose' piled the kids into the ranch pickup and headed up

Cottonwood Creek to the corrals to find a porcupine. As they approached the corrals there in the headlights was a young porkie stopped in the road blinded by the headlights just sitting there. Sean leaped out of the pickup followed by Rory and Stacy. The porkie started to run off the side of the road followed by the kids. The porkie headed up a tree when Sean caught up with it. The only way to handle these critters is with brooms. Sean knocked the animal off the bark of the tree and the three kids surrounded him and broomed him into the can. After they got the garbage can into the back of the pickup, they headed home bragging about how they were going to win the race. Rory even claimed the porkie could run the 100 yard dash in nine seconds flat. The porkie was left in the pickup in the can with the top tied down. Jose' drilled a few air holes in the top and they placed some porkie food and water in the can.

The next day Rory rode his bike to Sean's and Jose' and Jo-Bee drove them to the football field at the school. The crowd was getting bigger and lining the main street of Council for the parade.

When the parade was over everyone moved to the football field for the races. The crowd lined the football field and the kids came with their brooms and cans with the porkies in them. They all lined up in the end zone on the east end. Sheriff Rick was the starter. There were three kids on a team and there were ten teams. The object was the first porkie to cross the west end zone wins. The teams chase the porkies with their brooms.

Sheriff Rick said, "Get set. Go." And they were off. Sean, Rory and Stacy were team #3. There were huge porkies and team #3's was the smallest. They named him "Needles." Needles took off like greased lightning, only the wrong way. Needles headed right for the crowd on the North sideline. The kids caught up with him when he got to the sideline. Sean batted him back on the field. With Rory and Stacy's help they got him running the right way. Needles saw daylight at the end zone and out ran the kids. None of the other porkies got very far. Some ran backwards, some ran back to the cans they came out of. About half of them got half way down the football field, being broomed this way and that. Some just laid down. When Needles crossed the finish line, Sheriff Rick blew the whistle. They won 1st place. None of the others finished the face. The announcer ordered all porkies back in the cans. Sean, Rory and Stacy went to the announcer's stand to receive the trophy.

About that time a man in a suit and tie came to the stand and asked if he could announce something. He said, "I am from PETA (People for the Ethical Treatment of Animals). I think this event is deplorable. This will be your last year." The crowd went silent. Nobody, except Mr. O'Brien recognized this guy. He ran across the field to the stand and approached the man. Mr. O'Brien said, "You remember me. I am the lawyer when you tried to close the San Diego Zoo. I whipped your butt in court then and I will whip it again if needed. So I think you better leave and forget this whole thing. This is not California. This is the mountains of Idaho where the good ole boys live. Get a clue." The man then said, "Oh no, not you again." Sheriff Rick then escorted him to his car. He left.

Everyone clapped. Mr. O'Brien told the crowd not to worry. This event will go on for years.

The 4th of July was over. Things returned to normal. The weather turned dry, the rain had stopped. Haying season proceeded through July and August. It got hot and stayed that way. The kids were preparing for school in September.

The last week in August the winds started blowing over the hot desert in Southern Idaho and Eastern Oregon. The hot wind would hit the tall mountains of Idaho and form huge thunder clouds. Some had lightning and some rain. Most moved to the Bruce Church Wilderness to the North. Some rained over Council Mountain.

One night of the first week in September, just as the sun went down; thunderheads were forming over Council Mountain. About 9 p.m. as Sean was going to bed he could hear some thunder. He noticed that the wind was very strong coming out of the west blowing east toward Council Mountain. Just then the phone rang. Sean answered. It was Mr. O'Brien. "Your dad there?" Sean gave the phone to Mr. Conroy. Mr. O'Brien said, "There is a lightning fire

back up Cottonwood Creek that seems to be getting bigger. We're

going to need help." Mr. Conroy knew what was up. So he called

the smoke jumpers. Mr. O'Brien called the local fire department.

Sean said, "Can I go with?" "Yes, but do what I tell you to do." Sean

had put the silver cross in his toy box in his room after the wedding.

He knew it was good luck and he thought he might need it. He put

it in his pocket. They got in the pickup and went to the O'Brien

Ranch. Mr. O'Brien said I will follow you to the Cottonwood Corrals.

Mr. Conroy called home and told his wife that he has seen tall

flames leaping high into the night sky. He told his wife to call the

local Forest Service and tell them that we should set up a camp at

the Cottonwood Creek Corrals. She did. She then phoned Mrs.

O'Brien and told her to bring little Vickie to her house and bring

Licorice.

The wind grew stronger. Mr. Conroy thought that up by one

fire it may be at least 60 miles per hour or more. Rory got in the

O'Brien pickup with his dad and they all met at the corrals. Looking up the mountain they could see the fire being shifted by the strong winds. The thunder claps were getting louder and louder and lightning strikes were more frequent. Mr. O'Brien then turned to Mr. Conroy and said, "This is going to ruin all my summer pasture and maybe kill all my cows." Mr. Conroy said, "Let's head up as far as we can go to see if we can find some cows and open all gates we can reach." When they got to the lower gate some cows were standing at the gate. They let them out and the cows started, with their calves, down the road. They would gather them in the next week or so. The two men kept going higher up the mountain to find another gate but they were getting closer to the fire and winds kept changing direction, shifting back and forth.

Meanwhile the Forest Service, smoke jumpers, and volunteers from town and other ranchers arrived at the camp with picks and shovels. They were organized by the fire chief on where to clear brush, etc., to try to contain the fire. They started up the road and met the men coming down and they told them what was happening. Sean and Rory were still at the camp. They were told to stay put. Of course that did not work. They both grabbed an extra shovel and pick and headed in another direction where they knew there was a trail. The fire had gone to a crown fire and the winds kept changing. The boys not knowing what they were doing got a little too close to where the fire had worked south.

All of a sudden a big gust of wind that shifted the crown fire to where the boys were. The crown fire shot over their heads high up in the tall pines. Ash and sparks fell all around them. The boys dropped their pick and shovel and ran back down the trail as fast as they could. The wind shifted again and blew the other direction, shifting the fire the other direction. Sean grabbed the silver cross in his pocket and started praying. They got far away from the fire which stopped moving where they were. They ran all the way to the camp where some people from town were. Sean turned to Rory and said, "Boy am I glad that I brought the lucky silver cross with me. We could have been dead." Rory said nothing. He then noticed he had wet his pants.

Mrs. Conroy and Mrs. O'Brien arrived with others from town with food and water. Jose' and Jo-Bee drove them up to the corrals. It was very late at night now. The storm had moved on into the wilderness and had lost some of its intensity. When the fire reached the tree line high up on Council Mountain there was nothing else to burn. What had caught fire was still burning and was left to burn itself out. Crews stayed on duty for another week or so to make sure it stayed out. Both families went home the next morning exhausted and went to bed.

All over Council Valley neighbors and people from town caught and penned O'Brien's cattle. They soon got the cattle back to O'Brien's headquarters and got a count. They lost about 1/4 of the cattle – a big loss. The Conroy's and Big Mike also lost a few cattle; not as big of a loss.

School started and the boys went back to school life. They tried to return to normal. With the memory of the crown fire racing over head and fiery sticks raining down as they raced down the trail out of danger, and Sean holding the cross in his pocket. Sean did not tell anybody that Rory wet his pants and Rory damn sure didn't. Both kids and teachers let normal return to normal.

The cattle were out on the O'Brien's meadows where there was enough feed to get through fall. They put up enough hay to get through winter. A big discussion would be made in the spring. Mr. O'Brien had been taking review courses to pass the bar in Idaho and had taken the exam in August. He just got news that he passed. So he joined a firm in McCall.

A month after the fire the Forest Service informed Mr. O'Brien that his permit was canceled until further notice and that could be three to four years until the grass returned. The problem was the fire was so hot not only the grass burnt but also deep in the ground the roots were damaged. Trees were left as stumps or were burnt to ground level. Everything had to be replanted.

CHAPTER TWELVE

MARYLYNN AND CAROLYNN

One weekend in late fall Sean and Rory invited Stacy to join them and they asked Jose' to take them up the mountain to see the damage. Jo-Bee went with them. They drove up past the corrals to about where they started on snowboards the fall before. They all got out of the pickup and the kids went by themselves down to the cliff. Jose' and Jo-Bee went further up the mountain to see if by chance there were strays around. They agreed to meet back at the corrals.

When they got to the top of the cliff and looked over, they all said at once, "Oh my God, it's all gone." The ring of trees had disappeared. All that was left was a stump here and a stump there. None were more than one or two inches high. Most were burnt under ground level. By having the area fenced off for so long, much fuel built over the years which fed to the hot, hot fire. The three of them went down to the end of the cliff, then down to the front of the caves. Being late fall, it was time for the bears to hibernate.

They saw no bears or tracks anywhere. The kids wondered through what they thought was where the ring of trees had been. Sean knew more where the ring should have been but had to figure out where. The three made a pact, like they did before, not to tell anyone because who would believe them. They would not be able to find anything that looked like a ring.

Sean and Rory went into the caves a little way but found no signs of a bear. Just some old bones and some scat. Stacy started yelling at the mouth of the caves, "Sean, Rory come out look what is coming to the caves." Sean and Rory ran out of the caves to find what she was yelling about. Stacy pointed, "Look over there!" There were two very small black cub bears approaching the caves. Their mother was no where around. Sean said, "I wonder if their mother was burned up in the fire?" Rory said, "Let's catch them." So the boys ran after them. The cubs were very weak and could not run very fast. Sean grabbed one and Rory the other. They did not even put up a fight. Having dealt with sick calves both Sean and Rory knew what was wrong. They were not sick but starving. No mother's milk or having been taught to fend for themselves. The cubs were girls. They seemed very happy to see anything or anybody. Sean said, "We better take them home before the wolves get them. The fire chased most of the wolves away because the lack of food to hunt. The deer and elk were long gone. That didn't mean too much. The cubs needed attention. So the kids headed for the corrals. They met up with Jose' and Jo-Bee. Jo-Bee and Stacy cuddled the cubs like babies. Then Jose' said, "They're close to dying. They are very dehydrated." Jo-Bee answered, "Let's get home and get them food and shelter." When they arrived at the Conroy Ranch, Mr. Conroy met them at the barn. He said, "We need to call the vet first. Then I will get hold of Ranger Pete." The vet showed up almost immediately. He recommended warm milk first and then some berries. Ranger Pete with Fish and Game came a little later. He gathered everyone around and explained that we needed to jump through a lot of red tape if the kids were to raise them and he would do everything possible to make sure it happened.

The conversation then turned to what their names would be. Sean said, "Rose and Bettie." The cubs were both girls. Mrs. Conroy explained that the two doe that came to the ranch all the time to feed in the garden were Rose and Bettie. Mr. Conroy then followed with, "Sean, remember the two twins that lived near Gramma's house in Phoenix, Arizona that went to school with your Aunt Dottie? Their names were Marylynn and Carolynn." Sean answered, "Oh yea, that's cool."

The vet then said, "I know a nutritionist at the Phoenix Zoo, Dr. Freddie. I will call him." Jo-Bee asked if she could make the raising of Marylynn and Carolynn a school project. Ranger Pete said, "Boy, that will help alot for all of us to get through the State and Federal Government red tape." Jo-Bee then called Mrs. Bonnie on her cell phone and asked. Mrs. Bonnie said, "Great. Only you're not keeping them at school." The Conroy's agreed they would keep them in the dog kennel in the barn and Chocolate could stay in the house where he stayed with Sean most of the time. The vet suggested that until they get better they need to be kept warm.

Jose' said, "Jo-Bee and I have room in the bunk house." Jo-Bee commented, "Oh boy, now what, but OK." The deal was on.

The ideas bounced back and forth for another hour or so then they all went home. The cubs, Jo-Bee and Jose' and Chocolate's dog house went to the bunk house, the cub's new home.

The next day at school the news spread and everyone from students to teachers got into the act. There were field trips for every class to go to the Conroy Ranch to see the cubs. With love, care, the right food and the best habitat a cub bear could ask for, the cubs grew at an unheard of rate. From Ranger Pete, the vet, Jose' and Jo-Bee and all the kids especially Sean and Rory, the cubs were taught to lead with a leash and their new collars like puppy dogs. The cubs grew to love to be around the kids.

Ranger Pete jumped through all the hoops and they were granted permission to keep the bears for one year but then had to be returned to the wild. The trick now was to teach them how to survive on their own in the wild.

Winter was fast approaching. The cubs grew quite a bit until now. Then they started to slow down on their eating habits. They wanted to get in their dog house and sleep together, sometimes all day long. Jo–Bee explained to the kids that they were doing what bears are supposed to do; hibernate. She explained to the children that is how bears get through the winter when there was no food. The snow covers it all up.

As the cubs slept all winter, the kids after school rode the school bus to Little Hill or Brundage Mountain for snowboarding or skiing. When spring rolled around and the snow was mostly gone, Ranger Pete or the vet took the cubs out for training. Sean, Rory and Stacy usually went with one or the other.

One time when Sean and Rory went with Ranger Pete, Sean asked the Ranger, "Why did the Forest Service put the wolves back in the forest." Ranger Pete answered, "To balance the eco system." Sean asked again, "Who said it was unbalanced?" Pete answered, "Biologist." Sean asked, "Who are they?" Pete said, "People who study animals and plants." Sean asked, "You know the wolves killed some of our calves." Pete said, "Ya, I know, it's a long story Sean."

Ranger Pete has been with Fish and Game for many years, even

before they put wolves back into Idaho. He proceeded to try to

explain to the two boys that even though the studies done to

determine if wolves really needed to be part of our ecosystem, they

used places where very few people lived and wolves existed as a

control. Then they compared that to here where the wolves were

killed off 70 or 80 years ago. They then raised a lot of public

bleeding heart sympathy to get the people in Washington, D.C. to

give them money to re-introduce the wolves back into the Pacific

Northwest and elsewhere. He explained to the boys that for them

it was confusing. Their teachers told them they are essential to the

ecosystem but when it hurts their family economically they don't

understand. Pete told the boys he had a hard time also

understanding why the government does what it does. Pete then

explained how the squeaky wheel gets the grease and the golden

rule is that he who has the gold makes the rule. He went on to say only time will tell if the government made a mistake or if the government did the right thing. It was all up in the air.

They all got out of the truck and Sean and Rory let the cubs out of the truck. The cubs had their collars on and each boy hooked up their leashes. Off they went letting the cubs eat anything and smell anything they want. They had taken them to where they would let them loose at the end of the summer. Ranger Pete knew other bears were around this area all the time.

Pete motioned the boys toward the pickup. So Rory wanted to test Carolynn and took the leash off. She went running all around with Rory after her. Sean headed to the truck with Marylynn. Sean had to pull her because she wanted to be with Carolynn running around. Sean got her in the truck. Carolynn then turned and ran to the pickup and jumped right in. Ranger Pete having watched the whole thing was very pleased because he now knew that the two cubs would stick together and protect each other. Rory got back to the truck staying, "Boy is she fast."

All summer Sean, Rory, and the kids from school led by Jo-Bee took the bears up Cuddy Mountain on field trips letting the cubs get use to the habitat. Mrs. Bonnie told the whole school, 1 through 8, they had to write a paper on what they learned about the bears. She thanked God that Rory did not let them loose in the school. Jo-Bee was in charge of all papers. She thought the poem by Stacy was the best:

Roses are red, Violets are Blue

We learned from two bears, How about you?

We learned they eat berries and slugs

They eat beetles and bugs.

They don't have a mother But they play with each other

They act like two turtle doves

Even bears need love

Mrs. Bonnie declared her the winner. Stacy got bragging rights.

The end of August rolled around and the cubs were hog fat. Ranger Pete knew this was the time to turn them out on Cuddy

Mountain where they were taught to eat and play. Not Council

Mountain because the fire burned up the habitat. The cubs were

outfitted with radio collars so Fish and Game could follow their

movements. The bears were loaded in Ranger Pete's truck and the

three kids and Jose' and Jo-Bee took the bears up the mountain. As

they were going to turn the cubs loose, Sean took out the silver

cross and rubbed them both with the cross so they would have luck.

They turned them loose and said goodbye and then went home to

the Conroy Ranch.

CHAPTER THIRTEEN

TWO YEARS LATER – THE HOMECOMING

The Fish and Game kept the kids at school informed about where Marylynn and Carolynn were and what they thought they were doing. Mrs. Bonnie and Jo-Bee were pleased the students were able to have such a learning experience.

June 18th was Rory's birthday and the Conroy's had a small birthday party for him at their ranch. Just Jose', Jo-Bee, Sean, Stacy and some kids from school. Mrs. Bonnie also attended. It was a very sunny day – not hot, not cool. It was a typical birthday party. In June in Idaho the sun does not go down until very late, so it was high in the sky when they all had hamburgers and hot dogs with all the trimmings. Mrs. Conroy then brought out the birthday cake to the party on the big deck. They lit the candles, sang Happy Birthday to Rory as he blew out the candles.

Just as Rory blew out the candles, Mr. Conroy said, "Hey kids, look what just came across the river." They all stood up and looked. Across the hay meadow, two bears' heads were coming through the tall hay, bobbing up and down. They were headed to the barn. Mr. Conroy said, "All you guys stay put until I find out where they are going. The bears went into the barn through the back door unnoticed. The kids got off the deck and stood at the back yard fence. Mr. Conroy went around the barn to see if he could see if they were still in the meadow, not knowing they came out the other door.

Sean's eyes got as big as silver dollars and said, "Is that our bears?" Rory then said, "Look, they have collars on." Stacy then replied, "Each has two baby cubs with them." Sean leaped the fence followed by Rory and Stacy. Mrs. O'Brien yelled," Be careful." The bears went right up to the kids. The three kids yelled, "It's Marylynn and Carolynn. They have twin cubs each." The cubs stayed very close to their mothers.

Mr. Conroy came out of the barn behind the group. He said, "Call Ranger Pete. Tell him to come to the Ranch." Jo-Bee called him on her cell phone. The kids got acquainted with the bears all over again. Ranger Pete arrived right away. He called Fish and

Game before he got to the ranch. Fish and Game confirmed on the radio that reached the radio collars that it was Marylynn and Carolynn. The kids already knew that. No other bears would know that the kids were their best friends. Ranger Pete asked Sean to see if the babies were boys or girls. They all figured out that Marylynn had two boys and Carolynn had two girls.

There were some older apples in the fruit cellar so Sean got a basketful of apples and dumped them on the ground so the bears could have something to eat. They cleaned up the apples and then headed back through the meadow toward the river. Ranger Pete said, "I think they just wanted to show everyone their families." Jo-Bee and Mrs. Bonnie got lots of photos to show the kids at school. Rory asked if Ranger Pete thought they would come back next year. He answered, "Maybe if you keep feeding them apples."

Grass came back a little on the O'Brien permit, but the Forest Service limited what they could turn out. They told the O'Briens they may never get it all back. That was the word from headquarters in D.C.

Like a lot of small ranchers in the west, someone in the family has to have a job in town or another source of income. That's the only way to override the federal government restrictions and laws they keep putting on small businesses.

Sean and Rory did not pay much attention to what the government did. There were too many great adventures left in life to experience in the great State of Idaho. Some of the greatest adventures need lots of luck to experience. That's why Sean has kept the silver cross with the ring of trees on it.

Stay tuned. There is more to come.

Made in the USA
Charleston, SC
29 July 2012